Happy Birthday 3 year old

To Kyle from Grandpa &
Grandma Hults

Titles in This Series

My Alphabet Book
My Counting Book
My Book of Colors and Shapes
My Book of Opposites

LADYBIRD BOOKS, INC.
Auburn, Maine 04210 U.S.A.
© LADYBIRD BOOKS LTD MCMLXXXVIII
Loughborough, Leicestershire, England

Printed in England

My Book of
Opposites

by RONNE PELTZMAN RANDALL
illustrated by STEVE SMALLMAN

Ladybird Books

Jumbo is **big**.

Tiny is **little**.

At **night**, Jumbo and Tiny are fast **asleep**.

During the **day**,
they are wide **awake**.

Morning is breakfast time.
Jumbo gets the cereal
from the **top** shelf.

Tiny gets the
bowls from the
bottom shelf.

Tiny puts the bowls **on** the table.

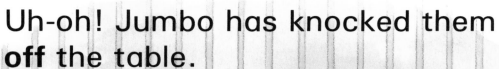

Uh-oh! Jumbo has knocked them **off** the table.

After breakfast,
Tiny and Jumbo do their chores.
They hang the laundry
outside to dry.

When it starts to rain,
they take it **inside**.

Jumbo's clothes go in the **tall** chest of drawers.

Tiny's clothes go in the **short** one.

The rain has stopped!
Tiny and Jumbo can go out
to play now.
Tiny's jacket zips up the **front**.

Jumbo's jacket has a buckle at the **back**.

Jumbo **pushes** Tiny **up** the hill.

Then Tiny **pulls** Jumbo **down** the hill.

Jumbo throws the ball
over the fence.

Tiny crawls **under** the fence
to look for it.

They have lost the ball!
Jumbo looks **up high** for it.

Tiny looks **down low**.
Who finds the ball?

Time for some ice cream!
Tiny has a **small** ice cream.

Jumbo has a **large** ice cream.

Jumbo is **big** and Tiny is **little** –

and they are best friends!